Amazing
Poisonous
Animals

EYEWITNESS JUNIORS

Amazing Poisonous Animals

WRITTEN BY
ALEXANDRA PARSONS

PHOTOGRAPHED BY
JERRY YOUNG

ALFRED A. KNOPF • NEW YORK

Conceived and produced by
Dorling Kindersley Limited

Editor Scott Steedman
Senior art editor Jacquie Gulliver
Managing editor Sophie Mitchell
Editorial director Sue Unstead
Art director Colin Walton

Special photography by Jerry Young
Illustrations by Mark Iley, John Bendall-Brunello, and John Hutchinson
Animals supplied by Trevor Smith's Animal World
Editorial consultants The staff of the Natural History Museum, London

This is a Borzoi Book published by Alfred A. Knopf, Inc.

First American edition, 1990

Manufactured in Italy   0 9 8 7 6 5 4

Library of Congress Cataloging in Publication Data
Parsons, Alexandra
Amazing poisonous animals / written by Alexandra Parsons;
photographs by Jerry Young.
p. cm. — (Eyewitness juniors; 8)
Summary: Text and photographs introduce poisonous animals such
as the fire salamander, death puffer, gila monster, and sea anemone.
1. Poisonous animals — Juvenile literature. [1. Poisonous animals.]
I. Young, Jerry, ill. II. Title. III. Series.
QL100.P36   1990   591.6'9 — dc20   90-31883
ISBN   0-679-80699-7
ISBN   0-679-90699-1 (lib. bdg.)

Color reproduction by Colourscan, Singapore
Typeset by Windsorgraphics, Ringwood, Hampshire
Printed in Italy by A. Mondadori Editore, Verona

Contents

Why be poisonous?

All animals have to find food and keep out of the way of other hungry animals. Some of them succeed by running fast; others have claws or horns or are good at hiding and keeping still. The animals in this book use another tactic: they make poison, giving their enemies some nasty surprises.

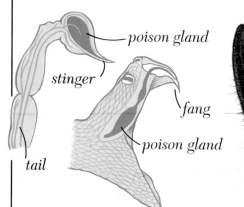

poison gland

stinger

tail

fang

poison gland

The scorpion makes a warning noise by rubbing its claws against its legs

A bite or a sting?

Animals are poisonous in different ways. Scorpions inject poison into their victims with special stingers on their tails. Snakes bite and inject poison with their fangs.

What are poisons and venom?

Any chemical that can harm or kill another living creature is a poison. Poisons that are made by animals may also be called venom.

stinger at end of tail

The imperial scorpion

The imperial scorpion (above) can be 5 inches long. It stings only if it is stepped on, or if it catches an animal that is too big to kill with its claws.

A sting in its tail

The scorpion hunts in the leaves and bark on the forest floor. It has big claws like a crab for grabbing insects. It arches its tail over its back, stinger quivering, and then it's goodbye, grasshopper!

Shall we waltz?

When scorpions court, they take one another by the claws and dance.

Hell's angels

Snakes, spiders, and scorpions have always been symbols of evil. The Egyptians worshipped the cobra, and some people have scorpions tattooed on their bodies.

A poisonous kick

There are no poisonous birds anywhere in the world. But there are a few poisonous mammals, such as the male platypus, which has poisonous claws on its ankles.

Small but deadly

Most poisonous animals are small. This little centipede could kill a mouse or a toad with one nip from its poisonous claws.

9

Arrow-poison frog

These tiny frogs live in the rain forests of South and Central America. Their bright and beautiful colors say one thing – Don't eat me, I'm poisonous!

The most deadly poison made by an animal...

....comes from the skin of the golden arrow-poison frog. One tiny frog the size of your thumb carries enough poison to kill 20,000 mice.

Terrible frog

This frog has no name in English. But its scientific name means terrible arrow-poison frog!

Poison for arrows

South American Indians dip their arrows in frog poison. Once a monkey or a jaguar has been scratched with a poisoned arrow, the hunters follow it through the jungle waiting for it to collapse and die.

Froggy family

There are more than 40 members of the arrow-poison frog family. Most of them are very brightly colored, and none are more than 2 in long - that's about as long as your middle finger.

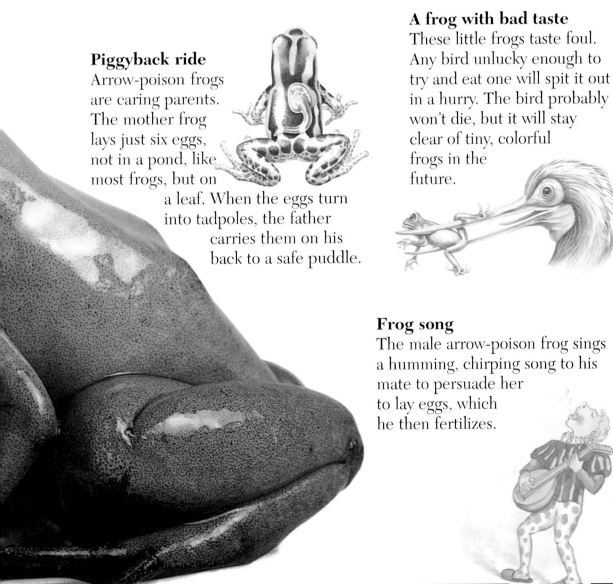

Piggyback ride

Arrow-poison frogs are caring parents. The mother frog lays just six eggs, not in a pond, like most frogs, but on a leaf. When the eggs turn into tadpoles, the father carries them on his back to a safe puddle.

A frog with bad taste

These little frogs taste foul. Any bird unlucky enough to try and eat one will spit it out in a hurry. The bird probably won't die, but it will stay clear of tiny, colorful frogs in the future.

Frog song

The male arrow-poison frog sings a humming, chirping song to his mate to persuade her to lay eggs, which he then fertilizes.

Deadly adder

The African puff adder is one of the world's deadliest snakes. It spends most of its time snoozing in the sand, waiting for an animal to stumble by. Then it strikes with amazing speed and sinks in its deadly poisonous fangs.

A gruesome way to die

The puff adder's poison makes its victim bleed on the inside. At first there is a burning pain around the wound. Then a huge bruise appears and the victim's lips begin to tingle. The poison can be fatal within half an hour or a few days.

layer of fake "skin"

fang

A splash in your tea?

Milking a puff adder is a little more dangerous than milking a cow. The idea is to make the snake bite a fake piece of "skin" so it will squirt its poison into a jar.

The poison is then used to make a puff adder antivenin, a special liquid for curing people who have been bitten by puff adders.

Colors blend in with desert sands

The Devil's poison

In one version of the Garden of Eden story, the Devil hides inside a snake's tooth. When the snake opens its mouth, out come the poisonous words of the Devil. He persuades Eve to bite the apple and commit the first sin.

Fangs a lot!

The puff adder has long fangs. But they're not quite as impressive as the fangs of the Gaboon viper (above), which can be 2 inches long.

Live ammunition

Roman admirals were known to throw jars of live poisonous snakes into their enemies' ships.

13

Stinging tentacles

The sea anemone looks like an underwater flower. But it is really an animal, with poisonous tentacles instead of petals. It uses its tentacles to paralyze fish and drag them into its huge mouth.

Fumbling for food

The anemone is always groping around with its tentacles. Each one is lined with thousands of tiny stinging cells, just waiting for a big fish or a big toe to come their way.

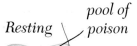

Resting

pool of poison

Whips of poison

When a fish touches a tentacle, the anemone's stinging cells are triggered. A tiny whip covered in barbs and poison comes lashing out of each cell.

barb

Triggered

Meet my friend

The clown fish (right) is not hurt by the anemone's poison. The two help each other to survive. The fish cleans the anemone and shares some of its food with it. In exchange the anemone lets the fish hide in its tentacles.

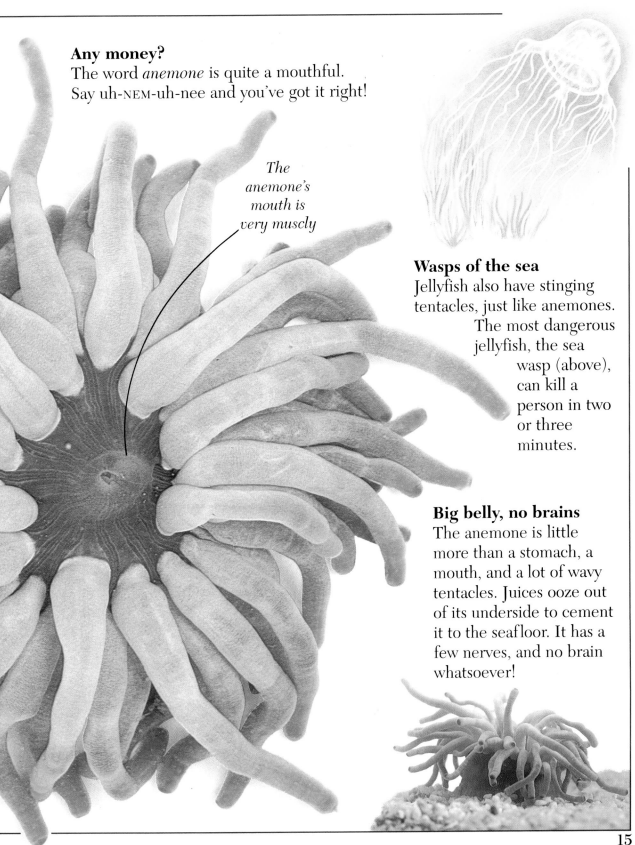

Any money?
The word *anemone* is quite a mouthful.
Say uh-NEM-uh-nee and you've got it right!

The anemone's mouth is very muscly

Wasps of the sea
Jellyfish also have stinging tentacles, just like anemones. The most dangerous jellyfish, the sea wasp (above), can kill a person in two or three minutes.

Big belly, no brains
The anemone is little more than a stomach, a mouth, and a lot of wavy tentacles. Juices ooze out of its underside to cement it to the seafloor. It has a few nerves, and no brain whatsoever!

Fiery salamanders

Birds, snakes, and shrews would all like a slice of salamander for supper. So these tiny animals have developed some nasty poisons to save their skin. And that's exactly where they store the poisons – in their skin.

Pretending to be poisonous

Some harmless animals have the same bright colors as deadly ones, so that predators leave them alone too. The red salamander looks just like the young of the deadly red-spotted newt, but it hasn't got a drop of poison in its body.

Red salamander

Young red-spotted newt

Salamanders from different places have different patterns of yellow and black

Not for hunting

Salamanders use their poison only for defense. When hunting, they rely on surprise and a quick bite.

poison gland

Fire salamander

The poison of this animal (above) won't kill you, but it would sting if it got into a cut. And birds don't seem to like the taste much.

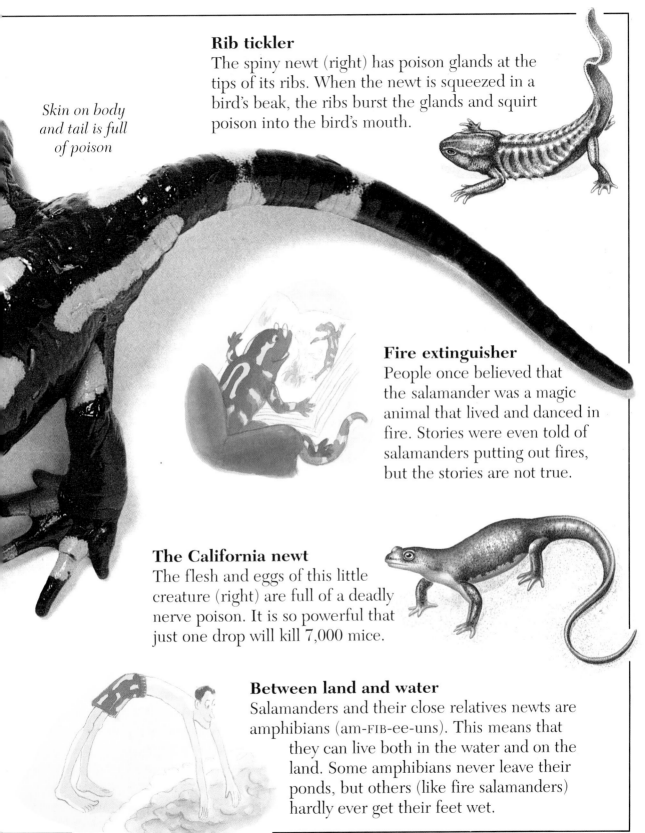

Rib tickler

The spiny newt (right) has poison glands at the tips of its ribs. When the newt is squeezed in a bird's beak, the ribs burst the glands and squirt poison into the bird's mouth.

Skin on body and tail is full of poison

Fire extinguisher

People once believed that the salamander was a magic animal that lived and danced in fire. Stories were even told of salamanders putting out fires, but the stories are not true.

The California newt

The flesh and eggs of this little creature (right) are full of a deadly nerve poison. It is so powerful that just one drop will kill 7,000 mice.

Between land and water

Salamanders and their close relatives newts are amphibians (am-FIB-ee-uns). This means that they can live both in the water and on the land. Some amphibians never leave their ponds, but others (like fire salamanders) hardly ever get their feet wet.

Death puffer

This tropical fish looks pretty harmless. But in its body is a poison more deadly than any snake venom. The poison can kill people in half an hour, by attacking their nerves so they can't move or breathe properly.

Lazy days
The death puffer swims slow and is easy to catch. It is only dangerous if it is eaten witho being prepared correctly.

Huff and puff
There are over a hundred kinds of pufferfish, and all of them have the same amazing talent. When they sense danger, they suck in water and blow themselves up like balloons.

Deadly dish
The Japanese are very fond of death puffer, which they call *fugu*. Chefs are specially trained to cut away the poisonous parts of the fish. But every year about 20 people collapse and die from *fugu* poisoning.

Blue-ringed octopus
This octopus (right) is one of the deadliest creatures in the sea. It injects its victim with a huge dose of TTX – the same poison found in the death puffer.

The death puffer's poison is found in its blood and in organs like its liver

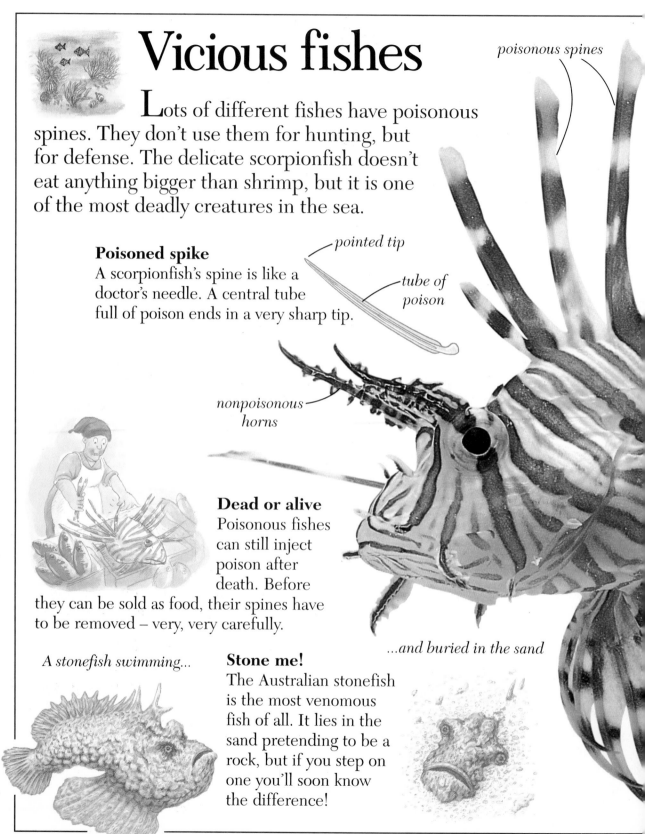

Vicious fishes

Lots of different fishes have poisonous spines. They don't use them for hunting, but for defense. The delicate scorpionfish doesn't eat anything bigger than shrimp, but it is one of the most deadly creatures in the sea.

poisonous spines

Poisoned spike
A scorpionfish's spine is like a doctor's needle. A central tube full of poison ends in a very sharp tip.

pointed tip

tube of poison

nonpoisonous horns

Dead or alive
Poisonous fishes can still inject poison after death. Before they can be sold as food, their spines have to be removed – very, very carefully.

...and buried in the sand

A stonefish swimming...

Stone me!
The Australian stonefish is the most venomous fish of all. It lies in the sand pretending to be a rock, but if you step on one you'll soon know the difference!

A sting from this beautiful scorpionfish can cause great pain

Saving energy

The scorpionfish (left) is found in warm, tropical seas. It glides along lazily, safe in the knowledge that bigger animals will let it be.

Open wide

Stingrays have been famous for their poison for thousands of years. The Romans even used their stings to stop toothaches.

stinger

Toxic toad

All toads are poisonous, and the giant toad is the biggest, ugliest, and and most dangerous of all. It uses the warty lumps on its shoulders to poison any animal that attacks it.

What an appetite!

Giant toads originally came from the Americas, but now they are found in Hawaii and Australia. Wherever they are they eat huge numbers of beetles, spiders, and anything else they can cram into their mouths.

A big mistake

Australian farmers imported giant toads to eat beetles that were destroying their sugar cane. The toads ate some beetles, but they also ate up everything else. Now they are a bigger problem than the beetles ever were!

Shoulder pads

A toad's poison glands bulge out around its head and look like shoulder pads. A cat or dog that ate a toad would get a mouthful of poison – and might die in an hour.

swollen poison glands

All toads have four toes on their front feet and five on the back

Toad carpet

There are so many millions of giant toads in Northern Australia that people sometimes look into their gardens and see not a lawn, but a shuffling carpet of toads.

The giant toad's skin and flesh are also full of poison

Croaking in peace

Male giant toads sit at the edges of ponds and croak to let their mates know where they are. They can be as loud as they like, because cats and dogs know to leave them alone.

What's for dinner, dear?

Roman wives were using toad poison to kill their husbands 2,000 years ago.

Gardener's surprise

All spiders bite, and all of them are poisonous. But some are nastier than others. The venom of the Australian funnel-web, which digs its den in people's gardens, can kill a person in less than two hours.

Injecting the poison

A spider's fangs are connected to glands bulging with poison. When the spider bites, it sinks in its fangs and gets a good grip with the help of special "teeth." Then it pumps its victim full of venom.

fang *tube*

poison gland

"teeth"

Giant killer

Most spiders eat insects, but funnel-webs have been known to prey on lizards and small birds.

A bad case of the blues

A nip from the funnel-web causes pain, cramps, and heavy sweating. Then the victim turns blue, froths at the mouth, and soon dies. In 1980 an antivenin was developed.

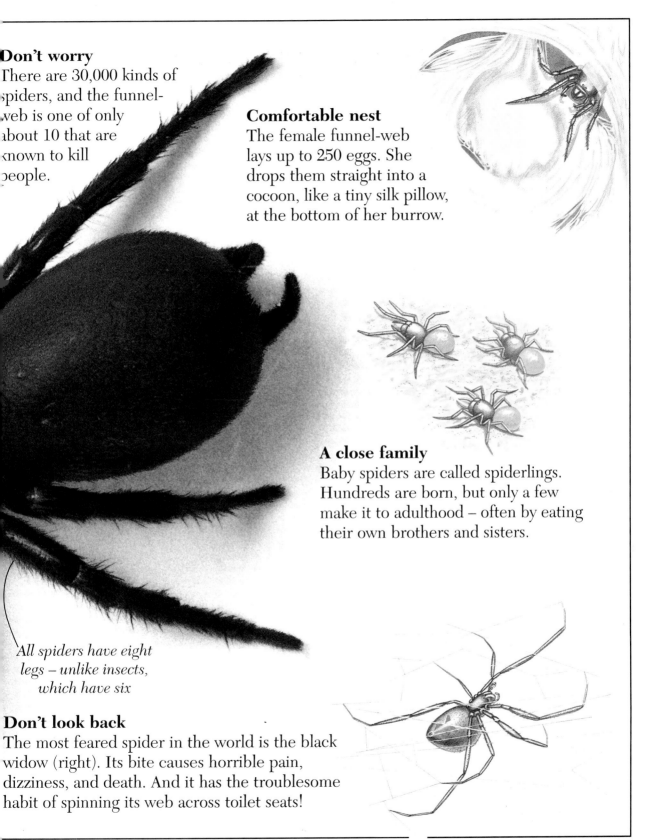

Don't worry
There are 30,000 kinds of spiders, and the funnel-web is one of only about 10 that are known to kill people.

Comfortable nest
The female funnel-web lays up to 250 eggs. She drops them straight into a cocoon, like a tiny silk pillow, at the bottom of her burrow.

A close family
Baby spiders are called spiderlings. Hundreds are born, but only a few make it to adulthood – often by eating their own brothers and sisters.

All spiders have eight legs – unlike insects, which have six

Don't look back
The most feared spider in the world is the black widow (right). Its bite causes horrible pain, dizziness, and death. And it has the troublesome habit of spinning its web across toilet seats!

25

Desert monster

There are only two kinds of poisonous lizards in the world, and this is one of them. It is called the Gila monster and it lives in the deserts of the United States.

Hello, cowboy!
This big, slow-moving lizard is named after the Gila (HEE-luh) River basin in Arizona.

A monstrous display
When a Gila monster feels threatened, it throws its head in the air and snorts and puffs like crazy. Its poison is mainly used for hunting, and sometimes in self-defense.

Brightly patterned skin warns other animals to stay away

strong claws for digging burrows

Fat tail
There isn't much to eat in hot, sandy deserts. So the Gila monster has to eat as much as it can whenever it can. It stores fat in its tail and can live off this for months or even years.

Groovy teeth
The monster's poison spills into its mouth from a gland in its bottom jaw. The lizard uses its special grooved teeth to chew the poison into its victim.

groove

Tooth

Bottom jaw

poison gland

Immunized
Many poisonous animals are immune to their own poison. This means that they can be bitten by another of their kind – or even bite themselves – without being poisoned.

Paralyzing poison
Drop for drop, a Gila monster's poison is more deadly than a rattlesnake's. It attacks the nerves and causes horrible pain and paralysis. Luckily, the monster rarely injects enough poison to kill a person.

Southern cousin
The only other poisonous lizard is the Gila monster's closest relative, the beaded lizard from Mexico (right).

Stings with wings

Bees and wasps are the poisonous animals you're most likely to meet. Usually their stings just hurt for a while. But a very few people are allergic to wasp or bee poison and can die from a single sting.

Domestic honeybee

The bee
Where would we be without bees? They fly from flower to flower, collecting nectar to make into honey. On their voyages they carry pollen from one flower to the next, which guarantees that fruits will grow from the flowers.

Wasps
Despite their nasty stings, wasps are also useful animals because they kill a lot of insects that destroy plants and fruit

This European wasp is one of at least 50,000 different kinds of wasp

Swarming

Bees live together in nests. When one nest splits into two, a huge cloud of bees leaves their home in search of a good spot to build a new one. This cloud of bees is called a swarm.

Stung to death

A honeybee's sting and poison sac are in its tail. When it stings a person, its barbed sting gets stuck in the skin. The sting and sac are ripped off and stay in the victim, pumping poison while the bee goes off to die.

poison sac

sting

Killer bees

A normal bee sting won't kill you. One boy was stung 2,243 times by an angry swarm and survived! But a new bee from South America has killed more than 150 people.

Spider slayer

Bees are vegetarians, but wasps are aggressive hunters that often attack bigger animals. A few kinds even kill and eat spiders.